Urban Anim.
of
Washington, D.C.

Isabel Hill

Star Bright Books
Cambridge, Massachusetts

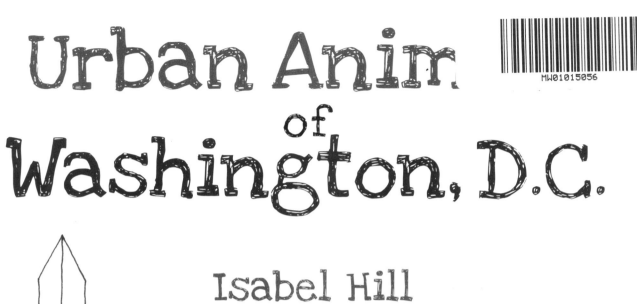

To my dear friend, Biba, who helped me explore, again, my former hometown!

Special thanks to my daughter, Anna, for her assistance in taking these photographs. —I.H.

Published in the United State of America by Star Bright Books, Inc.

The name Star Bright Books and the Star Bright Books logo are registered trademarks of Star Bright Books, Inc.

Please visit: www.starbrightbooks.com. For bulk orders, please email: orders@starbrightbooks.com, or call customer service at: (617) 354-1300.

Hardback ISBN: 978-1-59572-658-2
Paperback ISBN: 978-1-59572-659-9

Star Bright Books / MA / 00105130
Printed in China / WKT / 9 8 7 6 5 4 3 2 1

Illustrations by Catherine Hnatov. Copyright © 2013 Star Bright Books.

Library of Congress Cataloging-in-Publication Data

Hill, Isabel, 1951-
 Urban animals of Washington D.C. / Isabel Hill.
    pages cm
 ISBN 978-1-59572-658-2 (hardback) -- ISBN 978-1-59572-659-9 (pbk.)
 1. Decoration and ornament, Architectural--Washington (D.C.)--Juvenile literature. 2. Decoration and ornament--Animal forms--Washington (D.C.)--Juvenile literature. I. Title.
 NA3511.W3H55 2013
 729.09753--dc23
                        2013017715

The nation's capital has a secret to discover.

Animals are all around but some are undercover.

To find them, take a look everywhere,

On corners, in doorways, way up in the air.

UNITED STATES OF AMERICA

This art deco lamp stands outside

and gives the metal buffalo a place to reside.

On this pediment, there's a historical scene

with a cow, at rest, looking very serene.

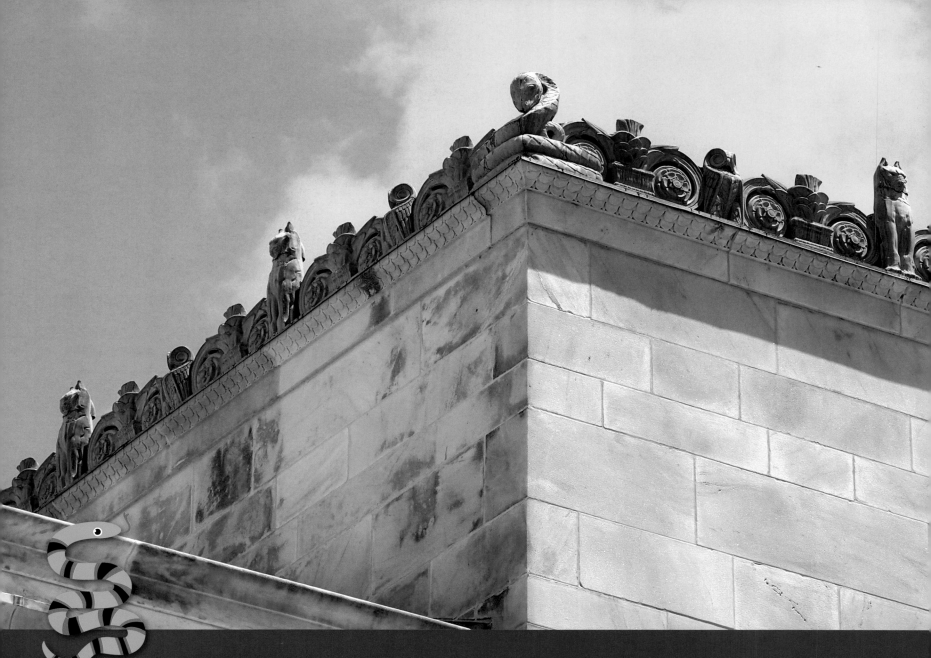

On the corner of this roofline there is copper cresting.

Will this snake strike or is he just resting?

Each rounded entrance has its own keystone.

A lion supports each arch on its own.

A special roof finial tells you right away

that a bear once lived here although not today.

The buttresses on this building make it stand tall.

The owls resting on them decorate each wall.

Architectural panels divide this building's face.

A curly-horned sheep helps separate the space.

Gargoyles take rainwater on a different route.

Here a frog's mouth is working as a water spout.

An architectural frieze goes all around.

You can almost hear the mules make a clip-clop sound.

In a medallion under dentils is a bird we all know.

The bald eagle—our symbol—makes a powerful show.

Pilasters on a row house are an interesting sight.

This dog on the front is guaranteed not to bite!

Animals on this relief are easy to see.

The fish carved in stone swim gracefully.

In a parapet over thin brick bands,

a peacock's feathers make a beautiful fan.

 On top of each column sits a giant toad,

below is a turtle that carries the load.

Perched atop this dentilled arcade,

four watchful parrots are on parade.

The sill on a window is a good place to rest,

for these elephants looking east and west.

A decorative molding ends with a stop,

It's a fierce-looking bat flying on top.

Wherever you go, look at each building's design,
Animals may be hard-but not impossible-to find.

Architectural Glossary

1. **Arcade:** A row of arches supported by columns.

2. **Arch:** A curved construction over an opening.

3. **Art Deco:** A style of architecture that uses simple, bold geometric shapes, such as circles, squares, rectangles, and ovals.

4. **Bands:** Flat, horizontal strips of stone or metal that split a building into sections.

5. **Buttresses:** Supports, usually in stone, built against a wall or projecting from the wall to help keep it from falling down.

6. **Column:** An upright structure, usually in the shape of a cylinder that supports a part of a building.

7. **Cresting:** A series of ornaments at the top of a roof or wall.

8. **Dentils:** Small, teeth-like square blocks.

9. **Finial:** A decoration at the top, side, or corner of a building.

10. **Frieze:** A decorative horizontal band.

11. **Gargoyles:** Carved stone creatures that project from buildings to throw rainwater off.

12. **Keystone:** A wedge-shaped stone in the middle of an arch.

13. **Medallion:** A circle or oval that looks like a medal.

14. **Molding:** A continuous three-dimensional band that is carved or applied to a surface.

15. **Panels:** Frames, usually in the shape of a rectangle, that are raised or set back.

16. **Parapet:** A low wall or rail that rises over the roof.

17. **Pediment:** A triangular-shaped space over a doorway.

18. **Pilasters:** Flat versions of columns, usually attached to a wall.

19. **Relief:** Sculpture or carving that extends out from a flat surface of a building.

20. **Sill:** The base of a window opening.

21. **Stop:** A carving used to complete the end of a molding.

Animal Habitats

U. S. Department of Justice Building
950 Pennsylvania Avenue, NW
Built: 1931-1934
Architects: Zantzinger, Borie and Medary
Designer: C. Paul Jennewein

U. S. Capitol, House of Representatives
East Capitol Street and 1st Street, NE
Built: 1916
Sculptor: Paul Wayland Bartlett
Architect: Thomas U. Walter

National Academy of Sciences Building
2101 Constitution Avenue, NW
Built: 1924
Architect: Bertram Grosvenor Goodhue

Russell Senate Office Building
Constitution Avenue and 1st Street, NE
Built: 1908
Architects: Carrere and Hastings

National Zoo
3001 Connecticut Avenue, NW
Built: 1907
Architects: William Ralph Emerson,
Hornblower & Marshall, Glenn Brown
and many others

Alban Towers Apartment House
3700 Wisconsin Avenue, NW
Built: 1928-29
Architect: Robert O. Scholz
Sculptor: Unknown

U. S. Department of Agriculture
South Building
14th Street and Independence
Avenue, SW
Built: 1930-1936
Architect: Louis A. Simon
Sculptor: Edwin Morris

Washington National Cathedral
3101 Wisconsin Avenue, NW
Built: 1907-1990
Architects: George Bodley, Henry Vaughan,
and Philip Hubert Frohman
Artist: Donald Miller
Carver: Constantine Seferlis

Pension Building
(National Building Museum)
4th, 5th, F, and G Streets, NW
Built: 1887
Architect: Montgomery C. Meigs
Sculptor: Caspar Buberl

**The Organization of American
States Building**
17th Street and
Constitution Avenue, NW
Built: 1910
Architects: Albert Kelsey and
Paul P. Cret

Row-house
1623 S Street, NW
Built: 1890
Architect: Unknown

National Wildlife Federation Building
1400 Sixteenth Street, NW
Built: 1989
Architect: Harry Barrett
Sculpture: 1960
Sculptor: Lumen Martin Winter

Sedgwick Garden Apartments
3726 Connecticut Avenue, NW
Built: 1932
Architect: Mihran Mesrobian

Reptile House, National Zoo
3001 Connecticut Avenue, NW
Built: 1931
Architects: Albert Harris and
Edwin H. Clark
Sculptor: John Joseph Earle

Apartment House
2101 Connecticut Avenue, NW
Built: 1927
Architects: Joseph Abel and
George T. Santmyers
Sculptor: Unknown

The Cairo Apartment Building
1615 Q Street, NW
Built: 1894
Architect: Thomas Franklin Schneider

Church of the Holy City
(Swedenborgian)
1611 16th Street, NW
Built: 1894-1896, 1914
Architect: Herbert Langford Warren